A CRY FOR HELP
And God Answers

Na'Tausha Clark

A CRY FOR HELP
And God Answers

Advantage BOOKS

Na'Tausha Clark

A Cry For Help… And God Answers by Natausha Clark
Copyright © 2018 by Natausha Clark
All Rights Reserved.
ISBN: 978-1-59755-424-4

Published by: ADVANTAGE BOOKS™
                Longwood, Florida, USA
                www.advbookstore.com

This book and parts thereof may not be reproduced in any form, stored in a retrieval system or transmitted in any form by any means (electronic, mechanical, photocopy, recording or otherwise) without prior written permission of the author, except as provided by United States of America copyright law.

Scriptures taken from the Holy Bible, New Living Translation, Copyright © 1996, 2004, 2007 by Tyndale House Foundation. Used by permission of Tyndale House

Library of Congress Catalog Number: 2018952315
1. Religion / Christian Life / Inspirational

First Printing: April 2018
18 19 20 21 22 23 24   10 9 8 7 6 5 4 3 2 1
Printed in the United States of America

Acknowledgments

I first want to thank my Lord and Savior Jesus the Christ for loving me when I didn't love myself. Lord I thank you for drawing me to you in my darkest hours and never turning your back on me. I thank you Jesus for being the very essence of love and teaching me how to release love to others.

This book is a manifestation of your saving grace in my life, and I give you ALL the glory for the testimony you have given me that will save others.

To my DREAM BIG editor, consultant, advisor and inspiration I thank you for giving so much of yourself freely. You exhibit the very essence of Matthew 10:8b (KJV), "Freely ye have received, freely give." May the blessing of the LORD continue to make you rich (in every area of your life), and add no sorrow with it.

With love to my daughters Breann and Tierra! I pray that this book will be the first glimpse of a great legacy and inheritance for you both. May you both be inspired to put GOD first in all that you do, and to live with purpose on purpose. The best is still yet to come. Love mommy!

To my Pastor, Dr. John R. Adolph, thank you for always encouraging me with your words and prayers of wisdom. Whether it was a personal prayer or a sermon you preached, GOD has used you to push me out of the shallow waters and out into the deep.

Thank you to my editors Kristi Powell (freelance writer and writing consultant), and Gail Showalter (author) for the time and energy you put into this project. I could not have done it without you.

A great big thank you to everyone who has prayed, prophesied, counseled, encouraged and loved me into this new place. I know if I list names I'll forget someone so if this pertains to you, Thank You!

FOREWORD

Abuse can occur to anyone of any age and gender and from any walk of life. It can take the form of physical battery, emotional bullying, psychological coercion, sexual abuse, or neglect. Domestic violence is an epidemic affecting individuals in every community, regardless of age, economic status, sexual orientation, gender, race, religion, or nationality. Domestic Violence National Statistics reports that three to four million women in the United States are beaten in their homes each year by their husbands, exhusbands, or male lovers. These reports state that one woman is beaten by her husband or partner every 9 seconds in the United States. These increasing figures are detrimental to society and change will only come when the brave have the courage to speak up and seek help.

For too long many have remained silent; hiding their experiences and turning away from valuable resources for help. I am both delighted and excited that my sister in the ministry, Natausha Clark has taken a stand and tackled this epidemic head-on. In her book entitled *A Cry For Help....And God Answers,* Natausha Clark boldly addresses the epidemic of Domestic Violence by giving an inside view of the life of a young girl who grew up with Domestic Violence at its center. The presence of Domestic Violence in this young girl's life has paralyzed her faith and diminished her morals and values. Abuse of any nature is a trick of the enemy. Whatever your situation, no one deserves to live in pain and fear. Whether you're the abused, the abuser, or a concerned friend or family member, use this book as your roadmap to VICTORY. Within each chapter, Natausha provides life-changing tools to reignite your faith and propel your life into the direction of living VICTORIOUSLY.

Thank you, Natausha, for your bold stand to serve as a change agent and speak up when so many others turn and look the other direction. I echo the words of the late Mahalia Jackson in the lyrics of her song entitled *"If I Can Help Somebody"* -

> *If I can help somebody, as I travel along*
> *If I can help somebody, with a word or song*
> *If I can help somebody, from doing wrong*
> *No, my living shall not be in vain*
> *No, my living shall not be in vain*
> *No, my living shall not be in vain*
> *If I can help somebody, as I'm singing the song*
> *You know, my living shall not be in vain.*

Natausha, this book is a reminder that your living shall not be in vain for your labor of love has helped somebody.

Rev. Arlicia R. Albert
Founder/Executive Director, MYE320 Speaker, Preacher, Author & Mentor
www.ArliciaAlbert.com
www.MYE320.com

Endorsements

Human hurt, abuse, and neglect are as real as the next breath that you will take. Rape, molestation, and sexual predators that strike from close range are often possessed with spirits of evil that can do damage that last a lifetime. But God, will always hear and respond to the cry of His people.

The transparency of Na'Tausha Clark is a blessing to the body of Christ. Her willingness to couple her personal pain with the truth of the printed promises of scripture are nothing short of amazing. This book is a must read for every Pastor who seeks to do effective ministry to those who have been wounded by sexual abuse; it is a healing balm for those who have suffered the indignity of being violated yet refuse to be victims but, have decided to be victors!

Clark is a victor and the journey that you will take in this text will prove to be life changing as she reveals her pain for the benefit of those who lack empathy, seek apathy and have refused pity to those that have been wounded but have seen the hand of God grant restoration like never before. Thank you Minister Na'Tausha Clark for allowing God to use your bruises to heal the brokenness of others.

Pastor, Dr. John R. Adolph, Antioch Missionary Baptist Church

When I first read *A Cry for Help And God Answers* I couldn't help wondering how many girls and young women are having the same experiences. Any woman who has been the victim of child abuse from a parent or sex abuse from a family member or friend needs to read this book. It is raw and realistic. Natausha Clark shows the reader how powerful faith is when releasing and letting go of the past.

Gail Cawley Showalter, Author of *Living Learning Loving*

Table of Contents

Acknowledgments 5

Foreword.. 7

Endorsements 9

Introduction 13

1: Crying Within.. 15
   (Childhood sexual abuse)

2: Crumbling On The Inside 23
   (Childhood mental and emotional abuse)

3: Running Away From It All 31
   (Childhood physical abuse)

4: Growing Up Too Fast 39
   (Teenage Pregnancy)

5: All Downhill 47
   (Rape and Domestic Violence)

6: Forgiving Leads To A New Beginning 55
   (The road to forgiveness)

7: Living Your God Chosen Life 65
   (Ruth's journey to true freedom)

Author's Remarks.. 71

Resource List 73

Natausha Clark

Introduction

This transformational book is a call to VICTORY for anyone who has endured abuse as a child or an adult and discovered the residue of the incidents left negative effects on his or her life. This book is written to encourage every reader to confront their past hurts and pains and be transformed by the renewing of his or her mind. After reading this book, you will no longer look at yourself as a victim but as someone who has gone through the major setbacks life sometimes offer yet come out VICTORIOUS! "A Cry For Help And God Answers" will take the reader through a young girl's journey of abuse from her childhood to adulthood. Each chapter provides a snapshot of Ruth's life and concludes with critical questions to help the reader overcome their pain and shameful past leading to a life of VICTORY!

For some, abuse is constantly plaguing their lives causing them to put themselves in new relationships that lead to more abuse. Most people who fall into this category find themselves in abusive relationships because it is familiar. Either they grew up in an abusive home, or they were entangled in bad relationships. Whatever the case may be you have to remember that you can't break the cycle of abuse by yourself. You must pray and ask the Lord to send wise counsel or a licensed professional to help you break free from the abuse that is plaguing your life. Another way to break an old cycle is read books and testimonies of others who broke through a life of trauma from abuse and are now living a life of victory. So instead of constantly reminding yourself of what you did not get right or what someone else has done to hurt you choose to forgive that person and yourself and MOVE FORWARD!

This book will remind you that no matter what happened in your past, life does not stop for you to catch your breath, gather your thoughts and recuperate. Instead, you have to make a decision to live your life in such a way, that you are determined to overcome your past hurt and pain and MOVE FORWARD to live a life of VICTORY! There is life after the pain. You can have an abundance of happiness, joyful relationships, and prosperity in every area of your life. Although you have gone through hard times and made some bad decisions, you don't have to allow the pain and shame of your past to hinder you from living a life of victory and freedom.

The situations that Ruth faced in her life were harsh and presented some eye-opening questions for one to consider, as a help to taking the necessary steps to the freedom of your future. Throughout this book, you will learn that it was Ruth's encounter with the God of all creation and His Son Jesus that helped to set her free from all the pain of her past. It was His transformative Word and her encounter with Him that changed her life forever. Even if you are not acquainted with the God of the Holy Bible, this book is still for you as it will help to open your mind and heart to healing that you may have never considered before. It's the healing power of Jesus Christ that will set you free, bring you peace, love, hope, transformation and victory! In His Word, you will be able to understand what His will and purpose are for your life, which will take you above and beyond anything you could ever imagine. As you read Ruth's story, listen closely to what the Lord may be speaking to you about letting go of your past hurt and letting Him restore you. Be open to receive healing as you journal your thoughts, read the scriptures and pray the prayers out loud, at the end of each chapter. Forgive yourself and everyone that has ever hurt you and watch God restore you to victory.

Chapter 1

Crying Within
(Childhood sexual abuse)

The clock has just struck midnight, and five-year-old Ruth and her mother are walking into Club Paradise. This club was no place for this beautiful, tiny, bright-eyed five-year-old but her mother could not find anyone to keep her, so she dragged her along. Innocent Ruth walked through the door of the brightly lit room, and the shiny lights made everything appear to be larger than they were. In Ruth's eyes, the pool table located in the middle of the room was as large as a swimming pool. She was too tiny to see over the top of the pool table, so she stood on her tippy toes to catch a glimpse of the green top and the scattered balls. Poor Ruth was not sure why she was the only child inside of the nightclub, and she was totally mesmerized by all that her innocent eyes witnessed. Her visit to Club Paradise was the beginning of Ruth's encounters of partaking in adult situations too early too soon.

Although Ruth was born to a seventeen-year-old mother, she was raised with the help of her grandmother, Mama Bell. In fact, the three of them lived together. Ruth's mother, Naomi spent the majority of her time partying with friends, so she left her in the care of her grandmother. When Mama Bell had to work, Ruth was left to spend the night with friends or family members. Ruth has fond memories of she and Mama Bell being snuggled up together watching *The Carol Burnett Show* and playing games together. Ruth knew without a doubt that her grandmother loved her because she spent so much time with her. The same things that assured Ruth that Mama Bell loved her also brought the same feelings that her mother did not want to be bothered with her. Naomi's inability to express love to Ruth was evident and spoke loud and clear to their loveless relationship.

Unfortunately, Ruth did not have very many pleasant memories of she and her mom. One of her worst memories occurred one night when her mother dropped her off at the house of a family friend so she could go out partying. Although her mother's friends lived there, Ruth knew it was a place she did not belong. Any time that Ruth was left in their care, they did not take care of her and treated her like she was an outsider. On one occasion her mother dropped her off, and in one night her life was forever changed. Everyone in the house had gone to bed in their bedrooms leaving Ruth to make the living room couch her bed for the night. Poor Ruth felt cut off, isolated, and shut out while everyone else slept in comfortable beds behind closed doors. Eventually, Ruth fell asleep in the open living room, but she did not have the entire room to herself. No one considered the idea of leaving a young girl asleep alone on the couch as open prey for a drunken man.

After being asleep for a while, Ruth was awakened by a bright light that found its way into the dark living room. Once the front door was opened, the light surrounded the image and Ruth recognized the drunk man as a relative of the family friend and at first she was not afraid. Although Ruth was not frightened by the man, something on the inside made her lay still on the couch hoping he would go into another room and find somewhere to sleep. Instead, her worst nightmare began to unfold. The drunken man made the couch his resting place right next to her. Ruth was afraid and in shock not knowing what do. Initially, she just laid

Chapter 1: Crying Within

there scared to move and immediately became paralyzed when the man began to touch her in ways her grandmother told her no one ever should. Even at the age of five, Ruth knew this situation was not normal, and she found the strength to move herself to the other couch, hoping to get away from the drunk man. Unfortunately, to her surprise, the man was drunk yet cognitive enough to follow her to the other couch and continued to touch her and caress her body as if she was a grown woman. Ruth's mind quickly began to wonder …….What is happening to me?…..Why is he doing this to me?…..Will anyone help me?….. Will anyone hear my cry for help?

Ruth felt helpless and did not know what to do. As quick as she could, Ruth got up from the couch and knocked on the family's friend bedroom door, but there was no answer, no help. No one came to her rescue. Ruth put her back against the wall and stood as still as she could hoping the man would not find her in the dark room. Unfortunately, she could not escape his grasp, and her innocence was taken away by a now fast asleep drunken man. Today Ruth remembers feeling like she was in a pit of darkness with an enemy there to defile her.

Ruth was frightened by the drunken man but found comfort in telling Mama Bell. Ruth knew her grandmother would protect her and she could tell her anything. Although she was afraid to tell Naomi what happened, her grandmother made her tell her mom anyway. Ruth followed Mama Bell's instructions believing that her mother would also protect her, but to Ruth's astonishment, Naomi looked at her and said, "You are lying!" Ruth's mother did not believe her and did not want to believe her because the drunken man was her friend. To hear Naomi call her a liar shattered Ruth's heart to pieces. Poor Ruth could not understand why Naomi made her feel like trash tossed in a dumpster. She felt betrayed and confused by the very person she believed would always protect her. Ruth could not understand why her mother would accuse her of lying. The words, "You are lying," cut her deeper than any perpetrator could and extinguished every ounce of trust she had in her mother. Those three words changed Ruth and Naomi's relationship, and after that day, the incident was never spoken of again by her mother or her grandmother. The man was never confronted and never received any consequences for his actions. At the fragile age of five, Ruth was crying on the inside, wondering why her mother chose to allow someone to violate her and get away with it. As a child, Ruth was waiting for someone to say, "I love you, I will protect you, and I will never let this happen to you again." However, that was not the case; no attention was ever given to Ruth, and she was forced to hold the trauma of her feelings, suppressing it all inside causing her to scream inwardly for help, wanting someone to tell her it was not her fault. But that never happened for Ruth. No one ever came to her rescue; no one ever offered her any love or protection. Instead, this five-year-old was forced to live the rest of her life suffering, with a silent cry, holding on to the memory of this trauma.

Consider This:

As you have read in this first chapter, Ruth had to experience childhood sexual abuse at a young age and face the reality that those who were responsible for protecting her would not be her protection. If you can relate to Ruth and her experiences, then like Ruth you must consider that you too may have been left with an inward silent cry. It is a cry for help and healing so that you can get over the pain of your past and move forward into your destiny and purpose. Take this moment to read and answer each question honestly. As you read the scripture and pray the prayer out loud your process of healing will begin.

So, how do you overcome the hurts and pains of your childhood and get healed from your inward cry?

Chapter 1: Crying Within

1. Face the reality of your pain.

Ask yourself if you are really over the pain from the abuse. Think back on the situation(s) in your life that have caused you the most pain, and if it still hurts you to think about it, then you may not be over it.

As the memories begin to flood your heart, journal what you are truly feeling inside.

_____

_____

_____

_____

_____

_____

_____

_____

_____

_____

_____

_____

_____

_____

2. Self-Examination.

Ask yourself if you have allowed the pain of your past to affect your present relationships.

Journal your thoughts.

3. Make a decision to forgive.

How do you feel about forgiving everyone involved with causing you so much pain? Journal your thoughts.

4. Scripture and Prayer.

Psalm 34:17-18 NLT, *"The Lord hears His people when they call Him for help. He rescues them from all their troubles. The Lord is close to the brokenhearted; He rescues those whose spirits are crushed".*

Lord, in the name of Jesus, I thank you for dying for me on the cross because by your stripes I know that I am healed. Forgive me for anything I have done wrong to hurt you or anyone else. I thank you for my life and for teaching me how to learn from everything that I have encountered. I understand that this pain is too much for me to carry, so I cast my cares upon You. Lord, heal me in areas where I hurt that can't be seen by others. Help me to trust you with my life, healing, and victory, in Jesus name. Amen.

5. Always consider seeking professional counseling or wise counsel!

Chapter 2

Crumbling On The Inside
(Childhood mental and emotional abuse)

Ruth's cry for help did not go away. In fact, the trauma of childhood sexual abuse continued to haunt Ruth. She had no one to help her nor did she have anyone to guide her. Ruth continued to harbor unpleasant memories and tormenting feelings of unworthiness. The miserable memories and feelings were suppressed inward and manifested into behavioral issues that would haunt her for the rest of her life. The feelings of fear, hurt and pain played a huge part in every decision Ruth made going forward. Unable to escape the trauma from her past, Ruth was forced once again to face the ugly demon of abuse, but his time from the hand of her parent.

Living with her grandmother was the one treasure Ruth found in life, but unfortunately, this treasure only provided an outlet for her mother to birth more children and stumbled upon a drug-addicted lifestyle. Her mother's hopes and dreams to move out of the ghetto were set aside, and she was forced to live in a low-income apartment with her children. Leaving Mama Bell saddened Ruth because she had become dependent upon her love and protection. Ruth was left to wonder who would protect her? Who would provide for she and her siblings while Naomi was out partying with her friends? Ruth was afraid to let Mama Bell know how terrified she was to have her life left in the hands of her mother. The answers Ruth searched for quickly became evident, and her life became worse than anything she had experienced.

It did not take long for Ruth's mother to start leaving she and her siblings home alone. Ruth was the eldest child and was responsible for taking care of her siblings. She recalls the days when Naomi would leave them in the apartment alone without enough food to eat. Now eight-years-old, Ruth would rummage through the empty cabinets and refrigerator searching for something to make a meal for them to eat. Once, the loaf of bread had become stale and hardened, but Ruth used it to make mayonnaise sandwiches because that is all they had to eat. Her care-taking duties did not end there. She had to comb her sister's hair and scrounge through the dirty laundry to dress everyone for school. Due to Ruth wearing smelly clothes to school, she found out quickly that abuse happens not only inside of the home but at school as well.

Living in chaos at home was bad enough, but now poor Ruth began to experience turmoil at her school. Other students began to bully her and make fun of her stained, smelly clothes. Ruth tried to make friends, but she was unable to overcome the hurt. She did not know how to respond to the hurtful words that were said to her, nor did she know how to ask others to look past her clothes and just play with her. Ruth could often be found sitting alone on one of the swings on the school's playground with her head down looking sad and lonely. The children would torture her at school and again when she got home. One day she went outside to play with some of the girls from school and instead of playing with her, they punched her and called her ugly names. With tears in her eyes and blood dripping down her face, Ruth ran home to tell her mother. Instead of her mother consoling her, she slammed the door right in front of teary-eyed Ruth. "Wait! Mom, I need you! Don't slam the door on me!" Ruth yelled out to her mother in desperation. Her little hands knocked and knocked, but her mother never answered. Ruth needed Naomi's love, but instead, she shut her out. Ruth sat on the porch waiting for her mother to open the door. She was not sure why her mother left her on the porch crying. Ruth thought to herself, was it because her mother's boyfriend was in the apartment with her, or maybe she disliked Ruth so much that she liked seeing her suffer? As she pondered this to herself, she also wondered, What did she do to make the girls treat her so badly? Even worse, what did she do to her mother to make her hate her so much? Unable to gain an understanding, Ruth was once again left sitting on the porch feeling alone, heartbroken and confused.

Consider This:

At a young age, Ruth had to bear the burden of mental, emotional, and physical abuse. And what hurt more than anything was to know that it all came from the hand of her mother. Ruth never told anyone about the pain she hid on the inside which caused her to feel heartbroken and confused. If you can relate to any of Ruth's experiences in this chapter and you have not had an opportunity to heal from the hurt and pain of your past, then you must realize that those feelings and past experiences are still stored beneath the surface of your heart. The reluctance to deal with these issues affects your decision making and interferes with every relationship in your life. It is important to be healed from all painful experiences of your past to move forward into a healthy future.

So how do you overcome the mental and emotional abuse you have suffered from the hand of others?

1. Face the reality of your pain.

Although emotional and mental abuse does not often show outwardly, the deep inner trauma can have long-term damages. Sometimes hurtful words from a parent or loved one can alter how you may feel about yourself.

If any memories pop up in your mind while reading this, begin to journal how you are truly feeling. Make the choice to release those negative thoughts and replace them with positive thoughts.

Chapter 2: Crumbling on the Inside

2. Self-Examination.

People who deal with emotional abuse also tend to deal with low self-esteem, have withdrawn personalities and are often unable to trust others. Ask yourself if you have allowed the abuse of your past to affect your present relationships. Journal your thoughts.

_____

_____

_____

_____

_____

_____

_____

_____

_____

_____

_____

_____

_____

_____

_____

_____

3. Make a decision to forgive.

Journal what your thoughts are about forgiving everyone involved with causing you so much pain. Began to speak the opposite of the negative words spoken to you.

4. Scripture and Prayer.

Psalm 147:3 NLT, ***"He (God) heals the brokenhearted and bandages their wounds."***

Lord Jesus I thank you for dying for me on the cross, and I know that by your stripes I am healed! Forgive me for anything I may have done to hurt you or anyone else. I thank you for hearing my hearts cry without me saying a word. Lord, there has been so much pain in my heart, and honestly, it has been too much for me to carry, so I give it all to You. Thank you for healing my broken heart and my inward and outward wounds. Now, help me to trust you with my life, healing, and victory, in Jesus name. Amen.

Turn your negative words into positive declarations. As a believer in Christ Jesus, you have a right to declare the Word of God over your life!

I am blessed and not cursed (Galatians 3:13-14; Numbers 23:20)
I am living a long and prosperous life and will not die an untimely death (Psalm 118:17)
I can do all things through Christ Who strengthens me (Philippians 4:13)
I am healthy in my body and strong in my spirit (3 John 1:2)
I have a crown of beauty for ashes and joy for mourning (Isaiah 61:3)

5. Always consider seeking professional counseling or wise counsel!

Chapter 3

Running Away From It All
(Childhood physical abuse)

No child should ever have to live in fear, but a life of fear and abuse became part of the norm for Ruth. For no apparent reason, her mother began to hit on her daily. She would hit and curse Ruth and poor Ruth never understood why. Day in and day out the abuse continued, and Ruth began to fear for her life. Ruth's daily prayer was that someone would help her get out of this horrible life in which she was forced to live. Little did she know that her prayers would be answered after an apartment below theirs caught fire and damaged Ruth's mother's apartment. The electrical and smoke damage was extensive and forced everyone that lived in the building out until the building could be repaired. As devastating as this was, it was an answered prayer for Ruth because she and her siblings all went to live with her grandmother until the building was repaired.

Months had passed waiting for the repairs on their apartment to be finished, and Ruth's mother did not like the delay one bit. Naomi hated living by Mama Bell's rules and having her mother see the life she was living. There were late night arguments as Mama Bell would tell Naomi to stay home with her children, but she refused. Ruth, on the other hand, loved it because it meant she had someone in her corner. She hated to see her mother and grandmother argue, but she learned to put a pillow over her ears and ignore it all. But one night the argument between Mama Bell and Naomi got out of hand, and in the blink of an eye, Ruth's mother found a rent house for them to move into. Ruth's mother packed their belongings and quickly left Mama Bell's home. Ruth did not want to leave her safety net, but she had to go.

At first, it appeared that the new move changed her mother, but boy was she wrong! It was not long before her mother returned to abusing poor Ruth. The beating and cursing made Ruth feel unloved and unwanted. She was tired of being cursed out, tired of being physically abused and tired of being used as a slave to take care of her younger siblings. To make matters worse, Ruth discovered that her mother was just a mean and hateful woman. One night Ruth and her siblings were in the bedroom playing, and her mother asked Ruth to close the kitchen pantry door. Ruth did as she was told and returned to the bedroom. Again, her mother demanded her to secure the pantry door. Ruth knew she had fixed the problem but returned to the kitchen to do as she was told. Ruth could not understand why the door would not remain closed. Curious Ruth stood back to determine what was preventing the door from remaining closed only to discover that her mother was intentionally reopening the cabinet door to pick on her. Naomi used the pantry door as a reason to scold Ruth. Instead of confronting her mother she kept her mouth shut and endured the beating Naomi gave her for the accusation of being disobedient. Shattered and broken by the thought that her mother was intentionally trying to hurt her, Ruth ran into a corner in her room and sat there curled up in a fetal position. Why was this happening to her? Ruth did not understand why her mother did not love her.

The only person that eleven-year-old Ruth ever felt any love from was her grandmother. Ruth prayed to God that one day she would return to live with Mama Bell. She did not know if the Lord would hear her cry, but she prayed anyway. Ruth promised the Lord that if he sent her to live with her grandmother, she would be a good girl. Ruth kept waiting, but the Lord was taking

Chapter 3: Running Away From It All

too long to fix her situation. She decided to take matters into her hands and fix the situation herself by running away from home, to escape it all. Ruth left the house running and was headed to her grandmother's house, but she never made it. She endured a panic attack on the way and was found laid out on the side of the road by an elderly couple. The couple questioned Ruth, but she was reluctant to explain what led up to her being there, so they dialed 911 for help. Ruth got help but not the assistance she wanted. After her runaway incident, a social worker was assigned to her family to make sure there was no evidence of neglect or abuse. The social worker was no help to Ruth, as a matter of fact, she noted Ruth as being a rebellious trouble maker and never investigated Naomi's behavior at all.

The lack of care and concern from anyone caused Ruth to continue to run away from home, in the hope that someone would hear her inward cry for help. Again, she ran to her grandmother's home, and this time she made it. Ruth thought, "FINALLY, I'm safe!" But no such luck, this time Ruth's mother showed up to Mama Bell's home with the police enforcing her to return home. Ruth's social worker met with her and Naomi and suggested that Ruth be placed in a group home, and that night she went to live in a home with other troubled teenagers. From the moment Ruth set foot into the facility, she knew she did not belong there, but there was a huge part of her that believed the Lord was answering her prayers. At least here she would not be beaten or abused and would find peace. From day one, Ruth quickly realized she was nothing like the other kids there. Most of the kids had endured conditions much like what she was experiencing with her mother, but what made Ruth different was the way she responded to the situations. The majority of the other teens had begun fighting, stealing, lying and initially showing signs of becoming promiscuous, however, that was not Ruth's case. Ruth held onto the values instilled from her grandmother. She had a hard time adjusting to living with kids who were rougher than her, so she had to learn to watch her back and keep her eyes on her belongings.

At this point in her life, Ruth did not believe that her prayers would ever be answered and she had nearly given up on God altogether. After spending six months in the Group Home, Ruth was released and allowed to return to her mother's home. The return to her mother's home was short lived. One last visit from the social worker changed everything. In fact, it was her mother's decision. She admitted to the social worker that she was dealing with drug addiction and mental illness. Her mother's truth was Ruth's gift from God. The Lord gave her the one thing she desired most, the gift to live with her grandmother. Finally, no more abuse. It brought joy to Ruth's heart to know that she would live with the one person she knew would love her and take care of her. She looked forward to living life as a normal kid and not as an abused child. By this time Ruth was thirteen, a young teenager that had already learned to bury the pain she endured beneath the surface of her heart. As a teenager, she tried to hide the pain of her past but little did she know that her pain was not hidden deep enough. Unfortunately, her pain had affected every area of her life, and it was just waiting for the perfect time to rear its ugly head.

Consider This:

If you have been a victim of physical abuse, then you understand the long-term impact it can leave on a person's life if the issues are not adequately addressed. Like Ruth, you may have tried to run away from the pain of your past or move away to a different city in hopes of getting far away from your abuser. No matter where you go the memories will follow you and affect your everyday life.

So, how do you overcome the childhood physical abuse you experienced from others?

1. Face the reality of your pain.

It is often said that a person should forgive and forget. However, this is easier said than done. Take this time to think back to any situation where you were previously abused. Be honest about what happened and as the memories begin to flood your heart journal your thoughts and true feelings. (If the pain is too much to bear alone seek a licensed counselor, wise counsel or someone you can trust that can help you through this process).

2. Self-Examination.

Often, prior abuse can cause a person to distrust others in any future relationships. The injured party can have a hard time building healthy relationships as he or she builds a wall to guard their heart in hopes to prevent reoccurrence of an abusive relationship.

Ask yourself if you have been allowing the pain of your past to affect your present relationships, and journal your thoughts.

_____

_____

_____

_____

_____

_____

_____

_____

_____

_____

_____

_____

3. Make a decision to forgive.

Once you decide to forgive the individuals that have hurt you, don't expect all of the painful memories to magically disappear. Allow yourself to go through the process of forgiving. This will take much prayer and a willingness to keep an open heart so that God can heal you over time. Journal your thoughts and how you are feeling.

_____

_____

_____

_____

_____

_____

_____

_____

_____

_____

_____

_____

4. Scripture and Prayer.

Isaiah 41:10 (NLT), *"Don't be afraid, for I Am with you. Don't be discouraged, for I Am your God. I will strengthen you and help you. I will hold you up with my victorious right hand."*

Lord, in the name of Jesus, I thank you for dying for me on the cross because by your stripes I know that I am healed. Forgive me for anything I have done to hurt you or anyone else. Help me to overcome the pain of my past as I go through the process of acknowledging the abuse and forgiving my abuser. Strengthen me as I move forward into a healthy and happy future. I thank you for taking the pieces of my heart and making me whole again. Now, help me to trust you with my life, healing, and victory, in Jesus name. Amen.

5. Always consider seeking professional counseling or wise counsel!

Chapter 4

Growing Up Too Fast
(Teenage Pregnancy)

Ruth was so excited to move in with her grandmother. Finally, she would be in a safe and healthy environment. After enduring such turbulent situations, moving into Mama Bell's home was one of the greatest gifts this thirteen-year-old could have ever received. Although it was a great gift, it was a gift that came a little too late. The damage to Ruth's self-esteem and self-confidence left her broken in so many pieces that Ruth became withdrawn, shy, and unable to make friends. Ruth wanted to make friends with the girls in her grandmother's neighborhood. She longed to share the giggles of the other girls. She thought that a new home meant everything in her life would be new; including new friendships but that did not happen for her. She met two girls in the neighborhood but felt that she did not measure up to be their friend. Ruth's life was nothing like the other girls. Both girls lived in two-parent homes, and it appeared that everything was perfect in their lives. When the girls talked about their dad's, Ruth would tell them that her dad was a police officer who was always around for protection. Although she was lying, she enjoyed pretending she had a father in her life. She would imagine him picking her up in his arms and holding her tight as he told her I Love You! The thought put a smile on Ruth's face, but on the inside she was sad, she longed to know, talk, and spend time with the man who was her father.

Ruth wanted a father-daughter relationship with her dad like the other girls had. She remembered visiting his parent's house but never spending time with him. Honestly, Ruth could not even remember how he looked. On her twelfth birthday, she recalls him calling to say happy birthday. Their brief conversation made her feel special and loved and her dad promised to visit her and bring a birthday present. Ruth was so excited to talk to him and to hear that he loved her. After their phone conversation, Ruth anticipated seeing him so that he could hold her in his strong, loving arms. Finally, she would have someone to love her. It was her heart's desire to be loved by her parents. But much like her mother, her father failed her too. That was the one and only phone call Ruth would ever get from the man she longed to have in her life. Ruth's dad never showed up with the gift he promised her or the love she anticipated. She felt abandoned and violated and made up her mind that she could never trust anyone.

Facing her truth hurt, and it forever changed her life. After the disappointment from her father, Ruth saw him as any other man, just another person that did not love her. The feelings of abandonment and unacceptance changed everything about Ruth. She longed for someone to hold her and say I love you, but that would never happen.

I love you. Three simple words that would mean the world for Ruth to hear never came from the most important people in her life. She had to come to terms with the truth: One, she would never hear those words from her mother because she abandoned her. And secondly, she would never hear those words from her father because he rejected her. Her grandmother's love was all that she had, and Ruth did everything she could to make Mama Bell proud. Ruth worked hard to be a good girl and prove she was not a failure. She tucked the hurt and pain beneath the surface of her heart, as she continued to walk her never-ending journey of sadness and despair. Poor Ruth had a difficult time separating herself from the trauma she experienced. Instead, she found it easier to be the class clown and not focus on her pain. Ruth liked the attention she would get from the other students and continued to say and do things to make them laugh. Her constant classroom disruptions left a bad impression upon her teachers and eventually led her to seek attention in all the wrong places.

One day Ruth met a guy, and she thought her search for "I Love You" was a thing of the past. Not only did this guy tell her I love you, but he also showed her the attention she longed for. Ruth's grandmother had talked to her about sex on many occasions and made Ruth promise to save herself for marriage. The last thing she wanted was for Ruth to also become a teenage mother. But a visit to the doctor's office confirmed Ruth's desire to be loved had turned into a broken promise to her grandmother. Becoming a pregnant tenth grader would by no means make her grandmother proud. Having to break the news to her grandmother was the hardest thing Ruth had ever done. Ruth's mother became pregnant at seventeen, and her grandmother begged her not to follow in the footsteps of her mother, but Ruth fell into the vicious cycle. Although Ruth disappointed her grandmother, she was elated that her "I Love You' man would be around to help her raise her baby.

Ruth's happiness was short lived. Mr. "I Love You" was only there for seven months of the baby's life. His secret drug life caught up with him one day, and after a court trial, he was sentenced to 20 years in prison. Now Ruth was left to be both mommy and daddy to her baby and her new responsibility consumed every part of her life. When she was not home taking care of her baby, Ruth was working at the local grocery store to provide her child with pampers, formula, food, and medicine. Ruth tried hard to do it all but working, going to school and taking care of a baby was too much for her. She missed a lot of school days and fell short on the required credits for graduation.

Ruth wanted nothing more than to finish high school and make both her baby and her grandmother proud by walking across the stage. She was unable to work, attend school and take care of her daughter with limited help. Her worse nightmare happened, she dropped out of school.

Consider This:

There were a string of events that led Ruth from one bad situation to the next. Abuse from her mother and rejection from her biological dad pushed her to look for love in all the wrong places. As a result, she had a baby at a young age and was unable to complete high school. Like Ruth, if you have made any mistakes that left you feeling like you have reached the end of your ropes, please know that it is not over yet. Even at the end of your rope if you just hold on you will find out that God can take your mess and make a masterpiece. Now is the time for you to stop blaming yourself for what you could have done differently and focus on making better choices that can create a better tomorrow.

Chapter 4: Giving Up Too Fast

1. Face the reality of your pain.

Take this time to forgive yourself for past mistakes. Let yesterday's failures stay in the past and seriously think about creating a better tomorrow. Begin to think about what programs you can get involved in that can help you move forward into a better and healthier future.

Journal your thoughts.

_____

_____

_____

_____

_____

_____

_____

_____

_____

_____

_____

_____

_____

_____

2. Self-Examination.

Acknowledge and rid yourself from any old behaviors or mindsets that could destroy any future opportunities. Journal your thoughts.

_____

_____

_____

_____

_____

_____

_____

_____

_____

_____

_____

_____

_____

_____

_____

_____

3. Make a decision to forgive.

It is sometimes easier to forgive others for what they have done to you. However, it can be even harder to admit your own faults and then forgive yourself. Take this time to forgive yourself for any mistakes you made throughout your life. Journal your thoughts.

_____

_____

_____

_____

_____

_____

_____

_____

_____

_____

_____

_____

_____

_____

_____

_____

4. Scripture and Prayer.

Philippians 3:13 (NLT), *"No dear brothers and sisters, I have not achieved it, but I focus on this one thing: Forgetting the past and looking forward to what lies ahead, I press on to reach the end of the race and receive the Heavenly prize for which God, through Christ Jesus, is calling us."*

Lord Jesus, Forgive me for anything I have done to hurt you or anyone else. Help me to let go my past failures and mistakes so that I can move forward to what lies ahead. I often feel inadequate and unable to achieve my dreams, but I know that I can do all things through Christ Who strengthens me. Open doors for me that no man can close, and close doors that no longer need to be open. I thank you right now for doing for me what I can't do for myself, in Jesus name. Amen.

5. Always consider seeking professional counseling or wise counsel!

Chapter 5

All Downhill
(Rape and Domestic Violence)

Ruth tried everything she could to run away from defeat, but defeat stalked her like Jason Voorhees from Friday the 13th. The very next year Ruth tried again to complete high school, but the parenting responsibilities were overwhelming. Ruth eventually dropped out of school for good and settled for getting her G.E.D. She wanted more than anything to be different than her mother yet ended up with a lifestyle that was a mirror image of her mother's life. Instead of trying to further her education by attending college or even a trade school Ruth hit the club life and began to party just like her mother did. Her baby's father was locked up, and she had no desire to sit around and wait 20 years for him to get out.

For years Ruth had an imaginary padlock on her heart. The abuse she endured over the years forced her never to trust anyone. She was unable to receive or give love until she met Tony. Tony was an older man that wanted more than anything to have Ruth in his life. In the beginning, Tony appeared to be a very nice man. He treated Ruth and her baby with lots of love and appeared to have a genuine concern for their future. Tony came into Ruth's life and made her feel special just when her self-esteem was at an all-time low. Eventually Tony won Ruth's heart, but it was not long before he revealed just who he truly was.

Ruth and Tony's relationship started out fantastic, but one day, Tony did a Dr. Jekyll - Mr. Hyde switcheroo on Ruth. While at a party Mr. Nice Older Man became jealous of another man complimenting Ruth, and in turn, he yelled and cursed at her demanding that she do not talk to other guys. It turns out Mr. Nice Guy was a drug dealing abusing thug! After he apologized to Ruth and assured her he would never hurt her again, Ruth decided she would stay with him. In Ruth's eyes Tony was her strength, her protector, and her provider; the qualities she had always wanted in a man. Ruth decided that she did not want to pass up the opportunity to finally have love in her life even if it came at the hands of an abuser. Tony was hard to figure out. Sometimes he was very nice to Ruth and other times he would get angry and become abusive. It did not matter what caused him to become angry; Tony would blame Ruth for everything. Ruth tried everything she could to make him happy and prove her love for him, but nothing was ever enough.

Ruth saw a very different side of Tony one evening while visiting his mother. The day started out wonderful. Tony introduced Ruth to several family members and a few of his childhood friends. Their family gathering turned into a fantastic evening with drinks, great food, and laughter. Everyone was having a great time until Ruth made a comment that Tony did not agree with. Right in front of everyone, Tony slapped Ruth so hard she immediately fell to the ground. She was stunned, shocked, and totally embarrassed. Ruth had never been hit by a guy before, but she recognized the same pain she felt when her mother hit her. Without asking any questions, Ruth grabbed her things and immediately left Tony mother's house. She had promised herself never to become anyone else's punching bag, so she telephoned Tony and ended their relationship.

The break-up only lasted about a week. Tony dropped by Ruth's house to apologize for his actions, and he promised never to hit her again. In the beginning, Ruth took a stand and refused to accept his behavior, but his persistence paid off. She forgave him and took him back. In Ruth's young mind she thought everything he said meant he loved her. Little did she know that his actions meant he wanted to keep her near him so he could control her and keep anyone else from having her. Tony made a strong comeback! Although he did not ask for her hand in marriage, Tony purchased a house for them to live in and nineteen-year-old Ruth became his "Shack-Up Queen"! Ruth thought the house would make their lives better but no such luck. She and Tony fought more than she had ever fought in her life. Ruth had experienced some of the most difficult situations any life could offer, but nothing she had encountered would even compare to the near-death situations Tony caused.

The worst night for Tony and Ruth happened after leaving a nightclub that she was not even old enough to be in. The night started out good, and they were having a good time until Big Rob walked in. Big Rob and Tony were frenemies that should have never been in the same room. No one knows what happened, but a fight broke out between them in the middle of the club, near the dance floor. People were frantically running away from the squabble as tables and chairs were scattered, and glasses were broken. Security broke up the fight, and the manager called the police. Tony and Big Rob left the building, but the fight was far from over. Tony and Ruth scrambled to get in the car and proceeded to drive off. They thought the drama was over, but the bullets fired at the car said otherwise. One of the shots hit their back tire, and the car was forced to come to a halt. By now the police arrived on the scene and began interviewing everyone involved including Ruth. The police discovered that Ruth was only nineteen years old and should not have been allowed inside of the nightclub. The interviewing officer pulled Ruth to the side to scold her for her actions and walked her around the car so she could see every bullet hole from the shootout. The officer then showed Ruth the bullet that entered the trunk and found its way into the back of a headrest that was behind her head. The police officer explained to Ruth that the trajectory of the bullet should have gone straight through the headrest and into the back of her skull. By all scientific accounts, Ruth should have been killed instantly. The reality of the entire situation was staring her right in the face, but she still did not want to accept the fact that she was in a dangerous relationship with Tony.

Ruth put up with Tony's cheating and physical abuse for another year and then decided it was time for her to move on. The only problem was, she had nowhere to go, so she continued to live with him to give herself time to plan her next move. Ruth began applying for jobs and low-income housing to get an apartment for her and her baby. Ruth stayed, but their relationship had taken a major turn, and they both began seeing other people. Although it should have made Ruth upset that Tony was with another woman, she was happy that Tony was seeing someone else. She thought things were going south with Tony until the night he came home wanting to have sex with her. Ruth said no, but Tony refused to take no for an answer. Tony slapped her across the head so hard that warm blood began to drip from her forehead down her face. Ruth knew this situation was about to get ugly, so she placed her baby safely into another room to keep her out of harm's way.

Ruth tried to get away from Tony, but he followed her into the next bedroom, grabbed her, pinned her down and raped her. She hysterically tried to free her arms to push him off of her, but he was too strong. With tears in her eyes, Ruth could not believe the man that once said he loved her was now raping her. Like everyone else in her life, Tony treated her like she was nothing. When he finally got off her all she could ask him was, "Are you happy about what you have done to me?" In response, Tony smirked and spat in her face before leaving. Ruth got up checked on her baby and then ran straight into the bathroom. All she wanted to do was wash his scent off. Ruth looked up in the mirror and did not recognize the girl who was staring back at her. She felt destroyed, humiliated, disrespected, and broken from the inside out. Ruth jumped into the bathtub filled with hot water and tried to wash away every hurt, pain, and disgusting, abusive moment in her life. Ruth did not even consider calling the police to report the rape; she did not think anyone would believe that the man she lived with raped her. Instead, she packed up everything she could leave with and began to run from her Nightmare on Elm Street.

Consider This:

Understand that the following statements are not that of a professional but from someone who has overcome traumatic events such as rape and domestic violence. These are two very sensitive subjects and should be taken seriously and handled cautiously. If you are a survivor of rape or domestic violence, take your time reading through this section.

Often the trauma of the event can be prolonged if the survivor does not go through the process of properly healing. How do you know if you have not properly healed? Here are a few signs…

If you still blame yourself for how your offender treated you, then you may need more time to heal.

If you relive the situation whenever something triggers a memory of the event, you may need more time to heal.

If you are unable to have a healthy relationship with someone of the same gender as your attacker, you may need more time to heal.

If you are fear-stricken to the point of not being able to do new things or travel alone without thinking that something bad may happen, then you may need more time to heal.

1. Face the reality of your pain.

If there's a flood of emotions and thoughts overtaking you as you read through this list, stop and Journal your thoughts.

2. Self-Examination.

Remember that your healing is not determined by the amount of time that has passed. It is important to get the proper help needed to overcome the lingering pain from the memory of the event. What are some ways you can go through the healing process?

Stop blaming yourself for what happened. Remember that what happened to you is not your fault.

Make the decision to press through the memories and allow yourself to heal. Wake up every day professing your liberation from the past.

Read books or testimonies of other people who have recovered from the pain of rape and domestic violence.

Journal your thoughts and feelings about the situation(s):

_____

_____

_____

_____

_____

_____

_____

_____

_____

3. Seek support groups in your community or church. Also from an online community or health professional.

Make a choice today to be set free from the pain of that event. Declare to yourself that you will no longer allow the pain of yesterday to affect another day of your life. Yes, the situation happened. No, you can't just forget about it. However, you can take away the power of that event by allowing yourself to heal and move forward.

4. Scripture and Prayer.

Isaiah 41:10 (NLT), ***"Don't be afraid, for I am with you. Don't be discouraged, for I am your God. I will strengthen you and help you. I will hold you up with my victorious right hand."***

Lord Jesus, I need you to set me free from the pain of my past. Heal my heart and deliver my mind from every hurt that keeps me in fear. Help me to know that you are with me. I need Your strength to help me through my healing process. Hold me up with Your righteous right hand, in Jesus name. Amen.

5. Always consider seeking professional counseling or wise counsel!

Chapter 6

Forgiving Leads To A New Beginning
(The road to forgiveness)

For six months, Ruth lived with her grandmother until she could regroup and get back on her feet. She found a new job as a janitor at a sanitation company and found an apartment for her to live in with her baby girl. It had been a long time since the last time she heard a word from Tony, but that surely did not mean he had gone away. One night there was a bad thunderstorm with heavy rainfall that beat against Ruth's apartment building. The evening news warned the entire community to stay in and weather the storm. It was late, and Ruth had no plans to leave the house for anything. She rocked her baby to sleep and climbed into bed to sleep the storm away. Ruth had only been asleep for a couple of hours when she was suddenly awakened by the sound of broken glass. She laid there scared to move and for a minute thought she was dreaming. She hoped she was only hearing things but no such luck, there was an intruder inside of her home. Ruth was awakened by her bedroom light that was flipped on by a man drenched in rainwater standing in the doorway of her bedroom. She began to scream as the man walked closer to her and she realized the man was no stranger, it was Tony. Ruth had not heard from Tony in forever. She was told he was in jail for selling drugs, but that certainly was not the case. Ruth came face to face with the truth; Tony was standing in her apartment with his eyes bulging, clothes soaking wet, looking like he was ready to start trouble.

Ruth realized her eyes were not playing a trick on her at all. Tony was very much inside of her apartment, and she was mortified. Tony stood blocking the only doorway that led out of her bedroom. He began begging her to please forgive him and give their relationship another chance. Tony begged but did not give Ruth a chance to reply. He immediately began running towards her yelling, "If I can't have you, no one else will!" Poor Ruth had no idea what Tony would do to her, and she found herself literally with her back against the wall. Ruth grabbed the phone on the bedside table and attempted to dial 9-1-1, but before she could hit the last number 1 on the dial pad, Tony snatched the phone cord out of the wall disconnecting Ruth from the possibility of anyone coming to her rescue. Ruth thought all hope was gone until she heard someone banging on the door. A voice yelled, "POLICE - Open Up!" Tony hid behind the door while instructing Ruth to open the door and tell the police officer that everything was fine. Ruth did as she was told but once the door was opened she ran out the apartment and yelled, "He's trying to kill me!" Tony surrendered without a fight and Ruth was finally able to breathe knowing that Tony would be taken into custody. The police officers interviewed Ruth and made sure she was unharmed before leaving.

Although Ruth was not physically hurt, she was an emotional wreck. The following evening she watched a Domestic Violence special on the local evening news, and she imagined herself as one of the women whose lives had ended in death. Those women were killed by their partners through brutal acts of domestic violence. Their stories and images haunted her. Tears begin to run down Ruth's face as she thought about what could have happened to her. She began to think about the many times her mother had beaten her for no reason and the times she was sexually abused at such a young age. She cried profusely thinking of all the times she could not defend herself at the hands of others. The more she cried, the more she realized that the God in Heaven her grandmother taught her to pray to kept her alive. There are so many things that could have happened that the Lord did not allow to happen and Ruth knew she owed her life to the Him and her grandmother. Ruth could not remember the last time she had been to church, but without hesitation, Ruth woke up Sunday morning, made her way to church and sat right next to her grandmother. Mama Bell quietly held her hand, and they worshiped together.

The Pastor entitled his sermon, "Whispers of Death" and taught a lesson that spoke to Ruth's heart. Although she had not been to church in a while, she remembered Mama Bell telling her that God loved her and he was a forgiving God. Her grandmother leaned over and whispered, "Go ahead honey, ask God to forgive you." Holding onto Mama Bell's wrinkled hand, Ruth took a deep breath and began to cry out to God for forgiveness. Ruth had not prayed in years, but none of that mattered. She knew God was real and she knew she needed him in her life to survive. Right there in church, Ruth asked God to heal her of the pain of her past. After service was over, Ruth went over to her grandmother's house for lunch. There was not very much conversation on the way home from church, but once they sat down to eat, Ruth's grandmother began sharing words to encourage Ruth to take the next giant step in her journey of healing; steps of forgiveness.

Forgiveness was a huge step for Ruth, and it began by acknowledging her past hurts and the pain it caused her. On the outside, Ruth looked like a woman made of steel. Regardless of the struggles she encountered in her life, she never allowed those struggles to defeat her. She was not defeated, but she covered up layers and layers of pain, hurt, and shame that was embedded deep within her soul. Ruth faced every struggle her life presented her with a thick skin. She always maintained a facade that nothing phased her when truthfully fear was tormenting her from every angle. Failure was Ruth's greatest fear of all. More than anything Ruth wanted her life to be different than her mother's. She did not want to become the expected young, uneducated black mother statistic that everyone labeled her as. Ruth knew that if she did not make changes in her life, she would end up on a dead-end street with nowhere to turn. Ruth decided to seek help and begin the forgiveness process.

Ruth arranged to meet with a Christian Counselor at the church. Admitting she needed help created a major shift in her life. The idea of allowing someone in her life to know her deepest secrets was something new and unheard of for Ruth. She was always afraid of being judged and afraid of being taken advantage of. Her fears caused her to keep her guard up and forced her to be quick to fight and even ready to pull a gun if necessary. Ruth possessed so much anger and rage in her life that if she did not confront it soon, she would either end up in jail or buried in a graveyard. The counselor began Ruth's healing process by making her identify everyone that had offended her in the past. This was a difficult step for Ruth. Ruth never realized it, but the counselor helped her discover a brick wall she had built when it came to forgiveness. Ruth wanted someone to be held accountable for the pain she endured, and she believed that by forgiving others, she would allow them to get away scot-free. Ruth believed that if she would let everyone else off the hook, then she would have to accept the fact that she was responsible for the decisions she made. This forgiveness process definitely would not happen overnight and would take multiple counseling sessions, time and energy from both Ruth and her Counselor.

Healing was indeed a tedious process, and Ruth's counselor was not cutting any corners. During their meetings, Ruth was forced to relive and confront every painful situation from her past including every one of her bad decisions. Ruth spent much of her

Chapter 6: Forgiving Leads to a New Beginning

free time on her knees asking God to release her from the pain that was suffocating the life out of her. Ruth met with her counselor every Wednesday for almost twelve weeks straight. She never realized it but the counselor's sessions not only helped her face the pain of her past but the sessions were also repairing her relationship with Jesus Christ. As she humbled herself to forgive others, the Lord was healing her heart from the bitterness she held captive. The more time she spent in prayer, the more she began to feel the love of God's only Son, Jesus Christ. Forgiveness gave her a feeling that she could not put into words. All Ruth knew is that she wanted more of it.

Ruth knew her counselor could help her find the answer to the more of God that she was seeking. In response to Ruth's request, her counselor suggested that she come to their sessions just thirty minutes earlier to give them time to study the Bible and learn more about a relationship with Jesus Christ. The thirty minutes was the best investment Ruth made in her life. She wanted to learn more about the Man that loved her in spite of the mistakes she made and she discovered He was the reason death was unable to take her life. Ruth rejoiced in knowing that the Lord surrounded her like a shield with his grace and mercy to protect her from all danger. She was no longer in any danger. Forgiveness freed Ruth from the bondage that held her heart captive. Ruth's decision to forgive provided a cleansing to her soul and opened her to a new life of love, peace, and happiness.

Consider This:

For many of you reading Ruth's story you may find it difficult to practice the old saying that says 'forgive and forget.' You may feel like if you forget about what your offender did to you, it is equivalent to him or her getting away with it. However, you are not being asked to forget… but to 'forgive.' You see once you make the decision to acknowledge the hurt someone caused you it does not stop there. You then must make a solid choice to let go of the pain and begin the process of forgiving that person and yourself, so that you can start your journey of healing. Understand that true freedom comes with a clear heart and a clear conscience. So once your heart releases the baggage that has been weighing you down, only then can you properly love and receive love from others.

If you are ready to move forward from the pain of your past, continue to read on and answer every question honestly.

1. Face the reality of your pain.

Write down the names of everyone who hurt you and list the things they did that caused you pain. Now make the decision to release them from your heart as you journey through the forgiving process.

Chapter 6: Forgiving Leads to a New Beginning

2. Self-Examination. Write down everything you blame yourself for; and ask yourself if you have been allowing the pain of your past to affect your everyday decisions and present relationships. Now journal your thoughts.

_____

_____

_____

_____

_____

_____

_____

_____

_____

_____

_____

_____

_____

_____

_____

_____

3. Make a decision to forgive yourself and those who hurt you.

Journal your thoughts about forgiving yourself and everyone who was involved with causing you so much pain.

4. Scripture and Prayer.

1 Peter 4:8 (NLT), *"**Most important of all, continue to show deep love for each other, for love covers a multitude of sins.**"*

Lord God, I am hurting from the event (name the event) of my past. I am broken on the inside, and I am unable to tell anyone about how I truly feel. Jesus, your Word says that love covers a multitude of sins, and I need your love to cover me and help me to break free from the pain of my past. I am ashamed about the things I was once involved in, and I need you to do for me what everyone else has been unable to do- LOVE ME THROUGH THE PAIN. Lord, heal my heart, my mind, my body and my soul, in Jesus' name.

5. Always consider seeking professional counseling or wise counsel!

Chapter 7

Living Your God Chosen Life
(Ruth's journey to true freedom)

Ruth was on the verge of walking into the brand-new start that she desired yet something was missing. She completed the required counseling sessions but did not feel like she was ready to move on. She released unforgiveness from her heart and restored her relationship with Jesus Christ, but still, something was wrong. For some reason, Ruth found it hard to move forward. She tried to live her life with new found freedom but had a hard time discovering what she would do next. Instead, she began to blame herself for making bad decisions that delayed the life she yearned for herself and her baby. Her self-blame built yet another wall of self-pity and caused Ruth to become withdrawn and again defeat set in. After the progress Ruth made in counseling, she couldn't understand why she couldn't find a better job that paid more money or a new house away from the low-income apartment where she lived. Ruth thought that just because she wanted a better life, it would fall in her lap but that wasn't the case. She returned to her counselor one last time and walked away with a renewed hope, after he reminded her that nothing changes overnight, and if she desired a better job and future she would have to work for it.

Ruth received a renewed hope that reminded her that she was created for greatness and that same greatness had been inside of her every step of the way. Ruth spent so many years crying about the pain of her past, but she never stopped to take a refined look at her future. Now that she was free from the drama of her past, she began to seek God in prayer about who He created her to be. She began making wise decisions to create a better future for herself and her baby. Ruth had always dreamed of graduating from college, so she took a leap of faith and enrolled. Not only was Ruth able to graduate with honors, but she also started her own business while working on a second college degree. The enemy did not make Ruth's transition easy; he always placed temptation in her path. It would have been easy to give into a life of negative behavior, but Ruth refused to let anything distract her from the goals she set for herself.

Determined to make her future greater than her past, Ruth took the advice of her counselor and wrote out long term and short term goals for herself. She had never identified goals for her life but with prayer and hard work she began to successfully see them through. Her relationship with her counselor taught her that she could not do this alone, so she began to surround herself with positive and successful people to make her journey a little easier. She discovered that there were people around her that wanted her to do well in life and would help her to stay on the right path. In return, she built new and healthy relationships that were based on success.

Yes, Ruth retains the horrible memories of her past and as much as she would love to forget it all, she can't. She has chosen to take the memories and allow them only to remind her how blessed she is. Ruth decided to release the pain of her past, focus only on the joy of her freedom and move forward into a better tomorrow. Not only did Ruth move forward successfully she also used her past to help other women with similar experiences to overcome their hurt and pain and move forward into a life of victory!

Consider This:

Chapter 7: Living Your God Chosen Life

Now that you have made a decision to break free from the pain of your past and start a new life, remember that change doesn't happen overnight. Commit to becoming the best you that you can be. No longer allow your identity to be based on what you have been through. See yourself as Christ sees you, as an overcomer, a victor and successful. Like Ruth, you must now think about the reality of your future and what you want it to look like.

Begin to create for yourself a better future by setting realistic short-term and long-term goals. After you have set those goals, begin to make the necessary steps to see them through. Remember to surround yourself with wise counsel and positive people who can help you meet your goals. And, when you see someone in need of help make sure to give him or her a hand up or lead them to someone who can.

1. List three short-term goals for yourself that you can accomplish in the next six months.

_____

_____

_____

_____

_____

_____

_____

_____

2. List three long-term goals for yourself that you can accomplish within the next five years.

Chapter 7: Living Your God Chosen Life

3. Now that you no longer identify yourself with the pain of your past, how do you identify yourself? How do you view yourself? Write a prayer asking God to reveal His purpose for your life.

_____

_____

_____

_____

_____

_____

_____

_____

_____

_____

_____

_____

_____

_____

4. Scripture and Prayer.

Jeremiah 29:11 (NLT), *"For I know the plans I have for you," says the LORD. "They are plans for good and not for disaster, to give you a future and a hope (an expected end)."*

Lord God, I want to thank you for everything you have done for me and what you have done for my family. I understand that without you I would have no future. I need you to show me the way and point me in the right direction. I don't know what is next for me, but I know that you do have a plan to prosper me and not to harm me, so Lord I need you to lead the way. Jesus, I owe you my life. Show me my purpose so that my life can bring you glory, in Jesus name.

5. If you need help to figure out what your next step should be, seek God's plan for you in prayer and consider wise counsel to help point you in the right direction! Remember to leave the hurts and pain of your past behind you, and daily make a decision to MOVE FORWARD into a life of VICTORY!

Author's Remarks

I am delighted that you have chosen to share in Ruth's journey from her life as a victim to victor! It is my desire to see everyone who has endured trauma at any point in his or her life to be set free from the pain of the past and Move Forward into their God-given destiny. Like Ruth, I too have endured horrible pitfalls in my life; however, I was able to pick up the pieces and place them at Jesus' feet. To tell you the truth if it was not for my encounter with the love of Christ, I would be stuck in my old life of misery. My breakthrough into freedom came as my relationship with Jesus grew through the Word of God, in the Holy Bible and the renewing of my mind.

If you noticed every chapter ended with a prayer and scripture, it is because I know that Ruth's story will encourage you, but only God and His Word can set you free. If you have not given your life to Jesus Christ or maybe you would like to rededicate yourself to Him. Read the following scriptures and prayer below that will lead you into a relationship with the only One, Jesus Who can take your life and make it a masterpiece.

John 3:16 New Living Translation (NLT)
16 For this is how God loved the world: He gave his one and only Son (Jesus), so that everyone who believes in him will not perish but have eternal life.

1 Corinthians 15:3-4 New Living Translation (NLT)
3 I passed on to you what was most important and what had also been passed on to me. (Jesus) Christ died for our sins, just as the Scriptures said. 4 He was buried, and he was raised from the dead on the third day, just as the Scriptures said.

Ephesians 2:8-9 New Living Translation (NLT)

8 God saved you by his grace when you believed. And you can't take credit for this; it is a gift from God. 9 Salvation is not a reward for the good things we have done, so none of us can boast about it.

Romans 10:9-10 New Living Translation (NLT)

9 If you openly declare that Jesus is Lord and believe in your heart that God raised him from the dead, you will be saved. 10 For it is by believing in your heart that you are made right with God, and it is by openly declaring your faith that you are saved.

Prayer: Lord Jesus, I believe in my heart that you died for my sin, was raised from the dead and is now seated at the right hand of God the Father; I confess with my mouth that Jesus is my Lord and Savior and I willingly surrender my life to you. Amen

Resource List

National Hotlines:

National Runaway Switchboard
1-800-621-4000

National Sexual Assault Hotline
1-800-656-HOPE

National Domestic Violence Hotline
1-800-799-SAFE

Child Abuse Hotline
1-800-252-5400

Women's Advocacy Project/ Family Law & Domestic Violence
1-800-777-FAIR

CASA/Court Appointed Special Advocate for Childcare
1-800-628-3233

Texas Hotlines:

STAR Program, Buckner Children & Family Services (Run Away Hotline)
409-861-0582 / 1-800-929-7828

Rape and Suicide Crisis Center
409-832-6530 / 1-800-793-2273

Natausha Clark is available for personal appearances or speaking engagements. For more information contact:

Natausha Clark
C/O Advantage Books
P.O. Box 160847
Altamonte Springs, FL 32716

NataushaClark@gmail.com

www.NataushaClark.com

To purchase additional copies of this book visit our bookstore website at: www.advbookstore.com

Longwood, Florida, USA
"we bring dreams to life"™
www.advbookstore.com

www.ingramcontent.com/pod-product-compliance
Lightning Source LLC
Chambersburg PA
CBHW051705090426
42736CB00013B/2544